Needle Poems

Needle Poems

Edited by
Anna Lisa Ohm

The cover features an *arpillera* [textile collage] made in 2011
collaboratively by the group Ocho Manos [Eight Hands] in Lima, Peru.
The arpillera depicts a high plateau in the Andes Mountains of
South America with local livestock of sheep and llamas;
waterfowl in the lake; and condors spreading their wings to the sky.
The tapestry is privately owned.
Book cover designed by Lisanna Paloma Design.

Needle Poems

You got to figure out which end
of the needle you're going to be,
the one that's fastened to the thread,
or the end that pierces the cloth.

-Susan Monk Kid, *The Invention of Wings* (337)

Acknowledgments

"Threading the Needle" was originally published by Larry Schug in *The Turning of Wheels: Poems*, North Star Press of St. Cloud, Inc., 2001. p. 29.

"NAIL POEM #14" and "NAIL POEM #42" were originally published by Larry Schug in *The Turning of Wheels: Poems*, North Star Press of St. Cloud, Inc., 2001. p. 64-65.

"NAIL POEMS #24, #38, #86, #37, #95, #89, and #9" were originally published by Larry Schug in *Nails: Poems by Larry Schug*, North Star Press of St. Cloud, Inc., 2011.

Dedicated

to

Lawrence "Larry" Schug

Contents

6

Introduction

The Minnesota poet Larry Schug's volume of poems titled *Nails* inspired his colleagues and friends to search for a feminine equivalent to the very masculine nail.

It's the needle, of course. For centuries women have been associated with sewing and weaving. For nearly as long, their contributions to art, history and culture were ignored or side-lined because of society's blind spot when it comes to valuing women's work, including needlework.

Public discourse is dominated by male speech, layered with such everyday expressions as to "hit the nail on the head," "another nail in the coffin," "dead as a doornail," or to "nail something," meaning to get it right.

Common expressions with the word needle may be fewer, but they are also widely used: look for a "needle in a haystack," to "be on pins and needles," or to "needle someone," meaning to annoy them.

An article about the intriguing process of superorditive designation, a device in the German language which devolves a masculine- or neuter-gendered word to a feminine, gave further intellectual foundation for Nail to Needle. Thus, the masculine *der Nagel* [the nail] becomes the feminine *die Nadel* [the needle]. So, the two words are directly related.

We are grateful to Schug for sharing his nail poems with the world and generating the inspiration for our response.

~Anna Lisa Ohm
Henderson, Nevada 2021

Part I

Needle Poems

Threading The Needle

To find (or lose) yourself
seek the place
you go where you go
when you thread a needle;
to the timeless, seamless place
where there exists only
the fingers on your one hand
holding the thread,
wetted in your mouth,
twisted to a point;
the fingers on your other hand
holding a needle
eye to eye,
breathless.

Only when the thread
passes through the needle's eye
do you return
to your turbulent, breathing life.

-Larry Schug

Needle Poem #6

Eyes can see, and
the eye of the needle
sees the thread coming
and sometimes ducks
because after that first stitch
the needle
can be tied down for a long time.

-Anna Öhmden

Alterations 2020

I. Hand-me-downs

I came to my family as third daughter in four years,
in a time where daughters were clothed alike.
Sometimes we shared just the pattern–
eldest in pink, next in yellow, and me in blue–
sometimes it was only the size that changed.

Third daughter gets the fun and fatigue
of clothes repurposed, recycled, hours of hemming
as sisters' clothes came down to me, school friends
mystified I could wear the same skirt for years
as I grew taller and broader and more myself.

When finances and family were torn apart,
hand-me-downs came from everywhere—charity
and foreign esthetic, not long-suffered favorites,
the rare leaven of vintage in a wardrobe
cobbled together to keep us going somehow.

I learned to sew in self-defense; fabric and patterns
economical back then, a seamstress could nearly match
the standard of the times. My choice of color and fit
with a dressmaker's dummy as my needle got clever
and sewing patched over the strained rents in the budget.

Not high fashion, but survival,
warmth, self-expression and the gentle
stubborn throb of the machine.

II. Haute couture

Silky fabric drapes over the dressmaker's form,
the surgeon of clothes extends an inspired and haughty open palm
as acolytes thread the needle,
      prepare self-buttons,
            rush to measure linings.

Elegant finished seams follow hidden patterns deep in the gown.
The garments of the well-dressed shimmer on the scant model
cheekbones and forward thrusting hips activate the dream of design
the great reveal of next year's collection–
      black or ochre or silk or tulle.

Pandemics challenge, threaten, offer a rare gift
of time to look in a new way, to see
the violence of rigid beauty and body images
      and scales fall from our mannequin structured vision.

Do we keep the same strictures
ask surgeons to remove a rib so we fit the dress?
Fatigued and proud, they'd hand us over to be closed up again.
We'd be riven with careful seams, scars that hint at
      the hidden dreams deep in the people.

Or would a tailor suffice, who can diagnose a funny slant of shoulder
and smooth our rough edges, create clothes that fit our bodies
      or illusions to hide the ways we do not fit the mold?

The truth begins with many fashion walks
beauty reimagined and unconstrained.
We could set aside the look and create space for comfort, health for all.
This could work—not high art but deep peace,
      not ready-to-wear but ready-to-survive, ready-to-thrive.

III. Alterations

A stitch in time saves nine. (Wisdom from the grandmothers.)

There is so much we cannot do but that needs to be done.
Healing and expansion must happen now.
We live a complex mending task—pick up the tools we have.
And I can sew, and patch, and recognize wear.

I can see a hand-me-down for what it is–
a garment made for someone else, passed on to me–
not my choice but what I have to work with to be clothed.
A hidden pocket in the silver lining of my struggle to find a way
to wear my own thoughts in the public sphere.

Would it help to let out seams, amend and repurpose
hand-me-down structures and systems that seem unalterable?
I hunt in my basket to find the right weight of connection
to thread the eye of the storm
and prepare for some serious repair.

Or are these seams that can't be let out anymore,
hems that are down to the thinnest line?
We are taller now. We can be more expansive still.
We need a stronger pattern that allows for movement,
for growth; a bigger garment—
we've always been so much more.

The grandmothers knew the power of stitches in time,
the courage and foresight of humble mending.
    This is the time.
    This is the time.

- Karen Lynn Erickson

Needle Poem #15

Quilting takes courage.
To plan ahead to fill the spaces
Stitch after stitch replaces
the repetitive thoughts that
pull one backward into self-defeat.
Quilting takes courage.
To make something useful to escape
the darkness of mental patterns.
Each pass of the needle making
new designs and vital connections
casting a lifeline to color and light.
Quilting brings comfort.

~Anna Öhmden

Patches

This is the day the Lord has made.
Let us rejoice and be happy today.

Happiness is a crazy quilt stitched every day
from scraps too good to throw away.
We've learned from our mothers' mothers how and why.

They knew we need the warmth of color on long cold nights
whether we lie together or alone.

Not that they thought about it much. No hard-working woman
spent her days sewing.
That was for the evening after the cows were milked,
the dishes done up, the bread set to rise,
when, by the light of the kerosene lamp
her children did their homework at the table
or someone played an old tune on the harmonica.
Only then did she pull out her needle and patches.

Crazy quilts were made to last, the stitches
tight and even, the fabric sound, the colors still cheerful
though muted by wear and washing and drying in the sun.

So too the quilt of happiness. You end every day
piecing together bright scraps--
the day's first laughter, the wren
making her nest of twigs and grass
in the end of the clothesline pole,
friendship remembered, sturdy, made of rough cloth.

But as fast as you can set in a new patch, happiness is undone–
        unstitched by the little hands of child slaves
        by the dimpled hands of the overweight boy,
        alone on the fringes of laughter,
                tugging his big T-shirt over his hips
        by hands gripping prison bars
        by hands throwing bombs at peace treaties
        made and rent in a day
                the edges frayed by exploding bodies.

Yet *This is the day that the Lord has made. Let us rejoice and be happy today.*

The choice, my sisters, is wrenching but clear:
surrender to the bitter cold
or take up our needles to stitch and stitch again.

                                ~Mara Faulkner, OSB

Needle Poem #18

A stitch in time saves nine.
But even if your stitch is late
it takes only a jiffy
to add another eight.

-Anna Öhmden

Needle Poem #5

Most of us needles are straight,
some of us are sturdy,
and some of us are fine.
A few have hooks at the end
For pearl one, stitch two.
Some are hypodermic
or phonographic
or magnetic.
But all of us are delicate and smooth.
And the classiest have great curves.
Did you ever hear of a surgical nail?

-Anna Öhmden

Needle Poem #12

Needles prick and stick and draw blood,
Needles mend and bend and upholster.
Needles tuck and trim and hem.
Needles knit and pearl and weave.
Needles prepare, puncture and inject.
Needles stich and hitch and patch.
Needles can excavate slivers, pop blisters,
    poke pimples, pierce earlobes 'n noses.
What would we do without needles?

-Anna Öhmden

Needlework

...but the needle travels
in and out
like a soul seeking new lives
always disappearing
then reappearing
reincarnating
in another stitch
that holds a life together

-Larry Schug

Needle Poem #18

Dedicated to Hans Christian Andersen

The emperor ordered new clothes,
the traveling tailors brought a cloth
so delicate as to be weightless
woven through with gold and silver threads
that remained unspooled,
cut with feigners' scissors,
stitched with threadless needles,
hung carefully on hangers
for the valets to dress his person
giving the emperor a lesson in vanity
by revealing the courtiers' stupidity.
A rich tapestry of words
reveals the most naked truth.

-Anna Öhmden

Needle Poem #9

I'm a needle.
Who are you?
Are you needling, too?

-Anna Öhmden

Needle Poem #16

Needles are dependable, if not abused,
and so is the cloth that has been used.
Wood rots and knots and splinters,
Cloth lasts through many winters.
The palimpsest colors fade in the sun
but a tight weave can't be undone.
A well-worn shirt takes on a silky feel,
rubbing when we bend and kneel,
causing elbows and knees to give way
to be patched and used for another day.
After thousands of years buried in the ground
A cloth of many colors can still be found.

-Anna Öhmden

Needle Poem #17

Dedicated to Johanna Spyri

In a rough-hewn wooden hut
in a remote alpine village,
just delivered of a son,
the mother needled for a name
in the Holy Bible
brought to her bedside
by the father's work-calloused hands.
Poking the sharp point
into an open page
it penetrated
deep into the Old Testament and,
where the needle left its final trace,
it reached back twelve centuries
to the palace of the Assyrian king,
Sanherib, whose name now lives on
in the newborn called Herbili.

~Anna Öhmden

Needle Poem #10

It is easier for a camel
to pass through
the eye of a needle
than for a rich man
to enter into the Kingdom of God.

~Luke 18:25

Part II

Needle Haiku

by Helen Rolfson OSF

Needle
HAIKU #1

Ouch! I stuck my thumb!
Filament led by steel rod
Lilliputian rope.

Needle
HAIKU #2

Did you get the point?
Yes, she said, you sew-and-sew.
You aren't what you seam.

Needle
HAIKU #3

With pins and needles
She fashions a woman's suit.
It's cooking with cloth.

Needle
HAIKU #4

I learned how to sew
When I was only seven:
"That's a woman's job."

Needle
HAIKU #5

She's sewing, stitching, basting.
Clothes are labor-intensive:
The price of needles.

Needle
HAIKU #6

A household treasure:
Humble needles cost so much.
Who would have thought it?

Needle
HAIKU #7

Pin money: what's that?
Money set aside to buy
A humble needle.

Needle
HAIKU #8

Deft fingers, sharp point,
Fingers were made to do this,
Bringing forth beauty.

Needle
HAIKU #9

Women: seamstresses.
Difference caused by a needle:
Men: couturiers.

Needle
HAIKU #10

Sewing is building.
Men aren't the only builders.
Needle: finest tool.

Needle
HAIKU #11

Mom did haute couture
For us on her old machine:
Converted treadle.

Needle
HAIKU #12

Leave home without it?
Never forget your needle
To rejoin frayed seams.

Needle
HAIKU #13

Symbol of union,
Needles reunite a world
Frayed at the edges.

Needle
HAIKU #14

Humble instrument:
Needle: insignificant;
Without it: bareness.

Needle
HAIKU #15

To avoid a war,
I think we should hide needles.
Who would fight naked?

Needle
HAIKU #16

It's criss-cross, criss-cross,
Stick needle in, pull it out,
Watch the pattern grow.

Needle
HAIKU #17

Brocade takes good eyes.
My needle's in; needle's out;
Beauty emanates.

Needle
HAIKU #18

They don't grow on trees:
Every bit of my clothing
Is work of needles.

Needle
HAIKU #19

Such a tiny tool
Needle's indispensable.
Every age needs it.

Needle
HAIKU #20

Pre-needle era
Was the Garden of Eden
Until skins and leaves.

Needle
HAIKU #21

They needed needles;
Adam, when he sewed fig leaves,
And Eve, robe of skin.

Needle
HAIKU #22

What's the point? She said,
Plying her needle in haste.
No one even cares.

Needle
HAIKU #23

Pre-sewing machine
Clothing was replete with frills
Now "simple" is rule.

Needle
HAIKU #24

The floor of pine woods,
Instrument of useful work,
Verb meaning "pester."

Needle
HAIKU #25

Needles, pins, thimbles,
Scissors, patterns, chalk and thread:
My construction tools.

Needle
HAIKU #26

My kit has needles,
Scissors, spools of colored thread:
All in case of need.

Needle
HAIKU #27

What's a needle?
A two-inch shaft with an eye
No camel can pass.

Needle
HAIKU #28

What is a needle?
A tiny-eyed metal rod
Kept in a haystack.

Needle
HAIKU #29

What is a needle?
As the nurse fills the syringe,
The patient winces.

Needle
HAIKU #30

What is a needle?
Being a diabetic,
Mother surely knows.

Needle
HAIKU #31

Needle under skin
Delivers good remedy.
Did you get flu shots?

Part III

Needle & Nail Poems

Needle Poem #1

That nail
That oh so male nail
So stiff and straight,
So tough and strong
so flat-headed.

That nail's been around awhile,
Been in, and out, and walked its mile.
I met #2, then #4—by the way, where's #1?

But I tell you
We needles are coming up fast, by gum.

~Anna Öhmden

Needle Poem #2

No one hammers a needle.
It makes no sense,
It's just not done.
You pick a needle up with care
    and
You never leave one lying there.

The point is sharp
It's made to penetrate.
A tiny prick draws blood
Unless the finger is nimble,
Or wearing a breast plate of thimble.

-Anna Öhmden

Needle Poem #4

Brother Nail
waits in the garage
in a coffee can
ready to be pounded
and put to use.

Sister Needle,
carefully sheathed in shiny foil
or stuck in a pin cushion,
waits in grandma's sewing basket,
already
threaded black or white
for a quick stitch.

-Anna Öhmden

Needle Poem #15

The naked needle
Stalked only by a thin thread
clothes others.

~Anna Öhmden

Nail Poem #24

I've been worryin' over
how a rusty old nail
like me,
a little dull,
slightly bent,
is ever gonna find work
when the line of nails
at the employment bureau
goes around the block,
and all these new nails,
galvanized, level-headed,
straight and sharp,
wearing identical
silver suits and hats
are looking
for the same job I am.

-Larry Schug

Needle Poem #7

The nail holds
the house together
on the outside
fighting board warp and rot
but a second use it has not.

The needle sets
her trap lines with thread
on curtain, chair and bed,
and saves herself
for another day.

~Anna Öhmden

Needle Poem #8

Old nails
compete with new nails.
New nails
compete with screws.
Needles have tenure.

-Anna Öhmden

Needle Poem #3

A nail,
whether new
or old and rusty,
is solid bodied and flat–headed.
A needle,
although ever so
delicate and fine,
nonetheless
has an open oval
all-seeing eye.

-Anna Öhmden

Needle Poem #13

for Maya Angelou

Jesus tells the truth
when he says
it is hard for a rich man
to enter the kingdom of heaven.
Indeed, it is easier for a camel
to go through the eye of a needle
than for a rich man
to get past the pearly gates.
Maya tells her truth
when she says
that when the camel tries,
it is the needle that gives
because the camel cannot.

~Anna Öhmden

Nail Poem #38

Driven
through the hands and feet
of a Galilean rabble rouser,
who could know
the future course
of the western myth
was hanging on us?

-Larry Schug

That Crown of Thorns

Who made that crown of
    thorns?
Whose hands could bend
    the prickly twigs?
Whose palms stay clear
    the needle-like thorns?
Whose fingers interlace
    the piercing branch?

Whose mind conceive
    such heady gear?
Whose mouth suggest
    such monstrous crown?
Whose eyes could seek
    the spiny bush?
Whose feet could carry
    them thither?

Whose stroke of irony
    spark the plan?

Who? Why?

What need could generate
    disgrace so deep
    astride already
    bleeding wounds?

-Anna Öhmden

Nail Poem #86

The magistrate's hands,
smooth though soiled,
washed of the matter,
never touch the hammer
that drives the nails.
Not only
are the hands and feet
of the prophet
bloodied,
but the magistrate
feels a need to wash
again.

-Larry Schug

Nail Poem #37

you can hammer
till you bend
a thousand nails,
you'll never
penetrate the knot
in some wooden heads.

-Larry Schug

Nail Poem #95

With proper instruction,
discipline
and meditation
a body can lie
on a bed of nails.
But no one
can lie on only one;
without fail,
a single nail
will impale.

-Larry Schug

Needle Poem #11

Would you rather be on pins or on needles?
Pins are like tiny nails, but sharp as needles
and too delicate to be pounded
on the head with a hammer.
Those who can lie
on a bed of nails
are foolish to try
a bed of pins or needles.

-Anna Öhmden

Nail Poem #89

The relationship
between hammer and nail
could be seen as confrontational
but when they put together
their iron heads
their relationship's co-operational.

-Larry Schug

Nail Poem #14

but the bent old nails
at the Veteran's Hospital
will tell you
that if a nail gets hammered too often,
its head breaks.

-Larry Schug

Nail Poem #42

The nail knows
he wouldn't've bent
if the guy had swung
the hammer straight,
but the guy just cusses
and tosses the nail away.
The nail knows
his only hope
is if some other guy
picks him up,
straightens him out,
makes him useful again.

-Larry Schug

Nail Poem #9

The universal law
of hammer and nail,
(as far as we know)
states that some cosmic hammer
pounds us a little deeper
into the ground each day
and we can't know
when the last hammer blow
has finally buried us
until the pounding stops.

-Larry Schug

Needle Poem #14

Did We Nail It?
Did we nail it, they ask,
needling me for a review.

-Anna Öhmden

Contributors

KAREN ERICKSON

Karen Lynn Erickson is a writer, composer, and professor
of French at the College of St. Benedict and St. John's
University, both in Minnesota. She teaches courses in
French language, literature, Biblical women and the history
of interpretation. She has always been intrigued by the
connections between poetry and music, and by the creative
ways human beings seek to understand and be understood.
With the Collegeville Consort, she released three CDs of
sacred medieval and Renaissance a cappella music. Erickson
is author of a chapbook of poetry, *Dwellings*, published by
Finishing Line Press, 2013, and founded an online poetry
project in 2016 with poet Mara Faulkner, OSB, *Caution:
Poetry at Work at CSB/SJU*.

ANNA ÖHMDEN

Anna Öhmden is Anna Lisa Ohm, Professor emerita for
German Studies at the College of Saint Benedict and
Saint John's University. Ohm specializes in 19th-century
and gender studies. Her translation of and scholarly
introduction to *Sina* by the Swiss-German author of *Heidi*,
Johanna Spyri, was published in 2020 in the Modern
Language Association's Texts & Translations Series, and
Bettine von Arnim and Gisela von Arnim Grimm's *The Life
of High Countess Gritta von Ratsinourhouse* in 1999 by the
University of Nebraska Press. Ohm's monograph on Spyri,
the first in English, *Johanna Spyri and Her Heidi: Newly
Reconsidered*, is in review. *Öhmden* in German means to re-do,
revisit, cut a grain field again, go back through again.

HELEN ROLFSON

Helen Rolfson, OSF, is Professor emerita of the Saint John's School of Theology and Seminary in Collegeville, Minnesota. Sr. Helen received her doctorate from the University of Strasbourg in France. She is currently chair of the Ecumenical and Interreligious Commission of the Diocese of St. Cloud, Minnesota. Sr. Helen grew up on a farm in Minnesota and as a member of 4-H completed many sewing projects. She still enjoys doing needlepoint. She became interested in traditional Japanese haiku poetry when a student shared a book about this art with her. Haiku's three lines of five, seven, and five syllables respectively is known for its needle-like precision.

MARA FAULKNER

Mara Faulkner, OSB, Professor Emerita of English, taught literature and writing at the College of Saint Benedict. In 2011 she received the Foley Prize for poetry from America Magazine. In *Going Blind: A Memoir* (2009), a Minnesota Book Award Finalist, Faulkner explores many kinds of blindness through the lens of her Irish ancestry, a family genetic diease, her Catholic faith, and ethnic groups in North Dakota. As a volunteer tutor, she has helped adults of many different ethnicities learn English. Other published books, *Still Birth* and *Protest and Possibility in the Writing of Tillie Olsen* are about poetry, and *Born of Common Hungers* about Benedictine women. Faulkner encourages readers to explore metaphors and to question their emotional and intellectual reactions to the written word. She currently leads writing workshops at the Spirituality Center of the Saint Benedict's Monastery.

LARRY SCHUG

Larry Schug is retired after a life of various kinds of physical labor. He currently volunteers as a college writing tutor and as a naturalist, though both activities have been curtailed by the pandemic. He has published eight books of poems, the most recent being "A Blanket of Raven Feathers," with North Star Press of Saint Cloud. Larry has won recognition for his poetry with three Central Minnesota Arts Board grants and a Loft-McKnight fellowship. He lives with his wife, Juliann Rule, two cats and a dog near a large tamarack bog in St. Wendel Township, Minnesota.

CPSIA information can be obtained
at www.ICGtesting.com
Printed in the USA
BVHW091548260421
605865BV00012B/2679